Philemon

FROM SLAVERY TO FREEDOM

CWR

Christopher Brearley

Published 2007 by CWR, Waverley Abbey House, Waverley Lane, Farnham,
Surrey GU9 8EP England. CWR is a Registered Charity – Number 294387 and
a Limited Company registered in England – Registration Number 1990308.
Reprinted 2011.

See back of book for list of National Distributors.

Unless otherwise indicated, all Scripture references are from the Holy Bible:
New International Version (NIV), copyright © 1973, 1978, 1984 by the
International Bible Society.

Concept development, editing, design and production by CWR
Cover image: iStockphoto.com
Printed in the UK by Page Brothers

ISBN: 978-1-85345-453-0

Contents

Contents

Introduction

A major part of the New Testament consists of letters. Most of these are addressed to churches and are generally rather formal, but a few are personal, written from one Christian to another. Paul's brief letter to Philemon, written about AD 60, is such an example. At first glance it would be easy to believe that this intimate letter about a domestic occurrence had little, if any, relevance to us today. This would be a mistake. The fact that it is included within the Bible and so a part of the inspired Word of God, demands our serious attention. Hence, what is its significance to our situation?

When reading the letter one observes that the outline is very simple. The chief concern is the fate of the slave Onesimus. He had run away from his master who lived in the Phrygian town of Colosse (or Colossae) in Asia Minor, to a city where he might conceal his identity amongst the crowd. This probably was the imperial city of Rome, though some commentators suggest it was Ephesus. The exact location is not important to this study. It is certain however that Paul was in prison in this city for preaching the good news about Jesus Christ.

As a result of divine providence, Onesimus came into contact with Paul, through whose ministry he came to faith in Christ (v.10). Not only that, it quickly became apparent that Paul was a dear friend and had also been instrumental in the conversion of Philemon (v.19), the slave's owner.

There is no doubt that Onesimus was a man of some ability and would have been extremely helpful to Paul in his ministry. There was also an obvious strong bond of affection between them and undoubtedly Paul would have liked to keep him not as a slave, but as a friend and a partner in the work of the gospel. First and foremost, however, it was vital for Onesimus to return to make amends for his previous bad behaviour. Encouraged by Paul, he returned to Colosse, accompanied by Tychicus and this letter which powerfully pleads for forgiveness on the basis of love that can remove all barriers. Onesimus should no longer be considered just a slave; he is now a beloved brother and should be received as such, irrespective of his previous failings.

Would these two men be reconciled – a slave owner and a runaway slave? Could such an appeal fail? We are not told, but Paul had the utmost confidence in Philemon. He says, 'Confident of your obedience, I write to you, knowing that you will do even more than I ask' (v.21).

Prior to studying this letter it is important to be familiar with some of the people involved. There are eleven mentioned by name, beginning with Paul, Timothy and Philemon (v.1). Then there is Apphia who is considered by many to be the wife of Philemon, and Archippus who may have been their son, or at least a close relative (v.2). Onesimus, the subject of the letter (v.10) is followed by Epaphras, Mark, Aristarchus, Demas and Luke (vv.23–24).

Paul, Philemon and Onesimus are undoubtedly the three principal characters and are, therefore, each individually studied in detail in the opening sessions. This should provide a valuable contribution towards understanding their feelings and the various difficulties which they faced. It will be seen that each one had to take a risk and make a sacrifice because of their allegiance to Christ. Using a personal approach also reveals how God can take ordinary people and transform them into something very different. Uselessness can be turned into the greatest usefulness by God's amazing grace.

Despite the difficult situation, the letter clearly portrays an attitude of thanksgiving and prayer. Paul is joyful, even though he's a prisoner, and active, for captivity did not prevent the progress of his missionary work. Nothing is impossible for a man (or woman) of God. He's also optimistic about his release and says to Philemon, 'Prepare a guest room for me, because I hope to be restored to you in answer to your prayers' (v.22). Whatever happens, he knows that his present sufferings, painful though they are, will be nothing compared to the joys to come which will last for ever (2 Cor. 4:17). Accordingly, Paul places his confidence in Christ irrespective of the present unpleasant circumstances.

The reader may wonder why Paul fails to question the rights of Christians to own slaves. Neither here, nor in his letters to the Ephesians (Eph. 6:5–9) and Colossians (Col. 3:22–4:1) does he appear to oppose the vile, degrading and loathsome practice of slavery. Quite the contrary, he sends Onesimus back and tells slaves to obey their earthly masters in everything they do. This is an important issue that requires thorough examination so as to understand Paul's true position. This letter provides the biblical answer to slavery and also the Christian way for tackling any form of social injustice. It is a message of love and reconciliation, applicable to every generation.

Are you ready for the first session of the Philemon study? Let me suggest that you carefully read and assimilate the whole letter which consists of only twenty-five short verses. Then enjoy the search to discover what God reveals through His servant Paul.

WEEK 1

Paul, a Prisoner of Christ Jesus

Opening Icebreaker

Discuss what characteristics you would expect to see in the life of someone who claims to be a Christian.

Bible Readings

- Philemon 1–3
- Acts 8:1–3
- Acts 9:1–19
- 2 Corinthians 11:16–33

Opening Our Eyes

Paul's letter to Philemon reveals a total transformation of character compared to that manifested when Saul (his Hebrew name) was walking along the Damascus Road uttering threats (Acts 9:1–2). Earlier he had given approval to the brutal murder of Stephen, the first Christian martyr. Saul was then actively involved in an extensive, energetic, violent campaign against the Church in Jerusalem (Acts 8:1–3).

Above everything, Saul was a man with deep religious convictions. He was a Pharisee, the son of a Pharisee (Acts 23:6) and strictly obedient to their many laws. These were incompatible with Christianity and a man of Saul's temperament could not tolerate rivals. So great was his opposition that he even pursued Christians who had fled to foreign cities (Acts 26:11). He was sincerely convinced that they were charlatans and blasphemers who were a very serious threat to the Jewish faith. Therefore, he was determined to suppress the infant Church using whatever means were necessary. Later he confesses to being responsible for the deaths of innocent men and women (Acts 22:4).

In Philemon, he goes from one extreme to another and pleads that a runaway slave, a Christian called Onesimus, be forgiven. Extreme prejudice and violent hatred are replaced by great humility and love. His career in blind religious fanaticism is replaced by an attitude of care and deep concern for the welfare of a former enemy.

Why the change?
Suffering teaches one many lessons that can be learnt no other way and can change people for better or worse. Sometimes it creates bitterness, resentment and self-pity, whilst it enables others to develop patience and perseverance (James 1:2–4) which lead to love and joy.

Certainly Paul had endured many trials: lashed, beaten with rods, stoned, shipwrecked, imprisonment and more besides (2 Cor. 11:16–33). Repeatedly he faced death in God's service and, like others, considered it a tremendous privilege. Suffering can make us more sensitive to the needs of others (2 Cor. 1:3–4).

Age can also improve people, and Paul was now an old man (v.9), somewhere around fifty-five to sixty years old, at a time when the average life expectancy was much shorter than it is today. Maturity softens most things in life, though not necessarily people. It can make them critical and selfish; alternatively, the rashness and faults of youth can be replaced by wisdom and tolerance.

Saul's conversion

Although he was undoubtedly influenced by suffering and age, there is only one answer to explain this dramatic change of character. It came as the result of a personal encounter with Jesus Christ. There are three accounts of his conversion, one by Luke (Acts 9:1–19), and others by himself (Acts 22:6–16; 26:12–18). Saul discovered that Jesus was God. He, who had persecuted those who believed in Jesus, would now endure much suffering for the name of Jesus. In his letter to Philemon he begins, 'Paul, a prisoner of Christ Jesus'.

If we live closely with someone we will inevitably become like them, if they are the stronger character. As Paul let Christ control his inner life, it influenced his outer conduct. God had chosen this most unlikely candidate to take His message to the Gentiles as well as to the people of Israel (Acts 9:15). It was when he began his ministry amongst the Gentiles that he preferred to be known by his Roman name, Paul. This once powerful adversary of the Christian faith now became its greatest advocate.

Discussion Starters

1. Why do extremists preach intolerance and hatred to exploit and oppress others? Differentiate between blind zeal and deliberate disobedience.

_____

_____

_____

_____

2. What are the differences between doctrine and indoctrination?

_____

_____

_____

_____

3. Saul was a Pharisee, the son of a Pharisee (Acts 23:6). How did this influence his character? What lessons are there for us to learn from this?

_____

_____

_____

_____

4. Why did Saul oppose Christianity so strongly? Think of situations where you may be provoked. How would you respond?

_____

_____

_____

_____

5. What evidence is there that Saul's conversion was due to God's initiative alone?

6. Discuss some of the ways in which people show prejudice today. Think of some examples from the Bible that teach us to be impartial.

7. Paul shows perfect tact in this letter. What does it teach about our attitude to others?

8. Paul begins his letter to Philemon by describing himself as 'a prisoner of Christ Jesus'. What does this mean for you in your situation?

Personal Application

God calls to His service some very unlikely people. For instance, Paul who was a great foe of Christianity became its greatest friend and endured many hardships for the sake of the gospel. Therefore, it should be remembered that someone who persecutes us today for our beliefs may one day be our brother or sister in Christ. This is a primary reason for loving our enemies and praying for those who persecute us (Matt. 5:44). Undoubtedly what is wicked must be denounced, for to seek peace at any price is not what the Bible teaches. However, there must be no attitude of revenge, rather the opposite. Loving each other is proof that we belong to Christ.

Seeing Jesus in the Scriptures

Paul says, 'I have been crucified with Christ and I no longer live, but Christ lives in me. The life I live in the body, I live by faith in the Son of God, who loved me and gave himself for me' (Gal. 2:20).

Once we have been united to Christ in His death our old life is ended; it would be foolish to suggest otherwise. Such an encounter inevitably means that we are not the same any more, for the old life is gone. A new life has begun (2 Cor. 5:17)!

To reform ourselves would be impossible, but God is able to transform our lives so that we become more Christ-like as the power of the Holy Spirit works within us. Knowing Christ means not only to experience His power, but also to share in His sufferings.

WEEK 2

Philemon, a Fellow-Worker

Opening Icebreaker

Philemon had a reputation as an encourager and refresher of the hearts of the saints. Think of examples of how you can be an encouragement to others. Share your experiences in the group.

Bible Readings

- Philemon 4–7
- Colossians 1:1–14
- Colossians 2:6–23

Opening Our Eyes

Nothing is known about Philemon other than that which we learn from the hints given in this letter. Even so, this reveals several important facets of his character which portray a favourable picture. He was a man of wealth and influence in Colosse and welcomed the church there to meet in his house. Whether this was the whole Colossian congregation or just a part of it is not possible to say. Archippus (v.2) was the local pastor (Col. 4:17).

At that time Colosse was experiencing a major economic recession due to trade having been taken away by the neighbouring cities of Hierapolis and Laodicea. Although these were extensively damaged by an earthquake around AD 60, it did not reverse the trend. Colosse never regained its former glory. As if this problem was not enough, persuasive false teaching had arisen which was leading people astray. Partly because of this Epaphras, a faithful minister of Christ (Col. 1:7), visited Paul in Rome. Paul's letter to the Colossians refutes these heresies and repeatedly stresses the superiority of Jesus Christ who alone is worthy of worship (Col. 2:6–23). Hence there were severe difficulties in Colosse when Paul wrote this letter concerning the relationship between Philemon and his slave, Onesimus.

Christian character

The brief description that Paul gives us of Philemon clearly shows his admirable qualities. He had love for all the saints (v.5) which is the fruit of faith (v.6). This was demonstrated in a willingness on the part of Philemon to show great generosity and kindness, hospitality and prayerfulness. He had often been a blessing to God's people. Such attributes are to be expected from one trusting in the Lord Jesus, and Philemon did not disappoint. Consequently, he's introduced to us (v.1) as a dear friend and much-loved fellow-worker.

Paul was deeply encouraged by Philemon's actions. He writes, 'Your love has given me great joy and encouragement, because you, brother, have refreshed the hearts of the saints' (v.7). To call him a brother indicates Paul's considerable love, high esteem and complete trust of Philemon. He's confident that Onesimus will be forgiven. Indeed, to refuse such a request would show that Philemon had not understood or benefited from God's forgiveness (Matt. 6:14–15).

Servile labour

One may be surprised to learn that Philemon, despite his many Christian virtues, employed slave labour. Is this not an obvious example of humankind's inhumanity towards each other? Does it not deny the fundamental truths of the Christian faith? How can loving your neighbour as yourself (Matt. 22:39; Mark 12:31) be reconciled with slavery?

It could be argued that it was an established, and therefore acceptable, common practice within society in ancient times. Also, although many masters were cruel, we may be reasonably sure that in a Christian household, slavery would take its least offensive form. However, this raises a further question. Is it ever right to do what is morally wrong so as to prevent a greater evil? In this instance, being a good master rather than a bad one? Such reasoning appeals to many but cannot be condoned. Two wrongs do not make a right.

What Paul tactfully teaches in this letter to Philemon and elsewhere is how to solve the difficult problem of slavery. The only solution is to inject love into the situation on all sides, masters and slaves. This vital principle is applicable today in solving social evils and is therefore carefully considered in the sixth study.

Discussion Starters

1. What are the characteristics of the Colossian Christians that cause Paul to rejoice?

_____

_____

_____

_____

2. To which problems in the Colossian church does Paul refer (Col. 2:6–23)?

_____

_____

_____

_____

3. What does Paul say about the ministry of Epaphras (Col.1:7–8)? What can we learn from Epaphras today?

_____

_____

_____

_____

4. The letter to the Colossians emphasises the centrality of Christ in the life of the church and in the lives of individuals. Why is this still crucial for Christians and churches today?

_____

_____

_____

_____

5. In what ways was Philemon a blessing to God's people?

_____

_____

_____

_____

6. '… faith by itself, if it is not accompanied by action, is dead' (James 2:17). Why is this?

_____

_____

_____

7. Philemon was a man of wealth. What are the advantages and disadvantages of this? Discuss how you feel wealth would influence your life.

_____

_____

_____

8. Can you justify Philemon employing slave labour? How should Christian masters regard their slaves?

_____

_____

_____

Personal Application

False teachers in Colosse were leading people astray.
Rather than placing Christ at the centre of their lives,
they were focusing attention upon themselves, their own
theories and ideas. In contrast, Paul never boasted about
his spirituality (see Phil. 3:7–8). Instead, he continually
taught that a personal relationship with Christ alone was
sufficient for salvation.

'See to it that no-one takes you captive through hollow
and deceptive philosophy, which depends on human
tradition and the basic principles of this world rather than
on Christ' (Col. 2:8). Those who dispute the centrality of
Christ, however plausible and attractive their arguments
may appear, are dangerous. They come in the name of
God, but in reality are messengers of Satan.

In what ways do Christians today face similar dangers and
how should they respond?

Seeing Jesus in the Scriptures

The Person and work of Jesus Christ, revealed in the
Scriptures, is the only true foundation on which the
Church can be built. 'For no-one can lay any foundation
other than the one already laid, which is Jesus Christ'
(1 Cor. 3:11).

Only a church built on such a foundation survives. Hence,
our sole motivation should be to make clear that the God
we love and worship is not *any* god. He is 'the Father of
our Lord Jesus Christ' (Col. 1:3).

Anything contrary to Christ's gospel must be opposed.

WEEK 3

Onesimus, a Runaway Slave

Opening Icebreaker

The practice of using slave labour flourishes in some industries today. Men, women and children are forced to work for little or no pay. Discuss how you feel about such exploitation and suggest what action might be taken.

Bible Readings

- Philemon 10–19
- Luke 15:11–32
- Matthew 18:21–35

Opening Our Eyes

Onesimus was a common slave – his name means useful.
No doubt it was given by the master in anticipation of
good service. Unfortunately, Philemon had found his
slave to be useless. The full nature of Onesimus' offence
is uncertain. Usually it is assumed that he had stolen
money or property from his master and then absconded
(v.18). Roman law ruled that whoever gave hospitality to
a runaway slave was liable to pay the slave's master for
each day's work lost. Could it be that Paul's willingness
to pay back any debt (v.19) is no more than to suggest
that he will make good any cost incurred by Onesimus'
absence? Had he been sent on an errand to Paul and
overstayed his time? Whatever the circumstances, he is
certainly guilty of being absent without permission.

In a Christian household like that of Philemon, you
would assume that Onesimus had often heard the gospel
message and experienced Christian love. Why then should
he run away? Had he committed some serious offence
and feared detection and punishment? Or was he tempted
by the taste of freedom? Satan's common strategy is to
lead one astray by making that which is sinful appear to
be desirable.

Running away was a serious mistake. Probably any stolen
money would soon be spent and he would be forced to
endure misery and squalor in the city slums. Besides this
he would have to be constantly careful to conceal his
true identity and background. Like the 'Lost Son' (Luke
15:11–32), he may have longed to return and enjoy the
comforts he once had. Did this desperate fugitive come to
his senses and seek Paul, having heard his master speak
of him with great affection? Had he been arrested and,
by the grace of God, become a fellow prisoner? It is not
possible to know, other than that they met. Onesimus
also met Paul's Saviour, for he came to faith in Christ.

Now he is a changed man and so Paul can confidently write, 'Formerly he was useless to you, but now he has become useful both to you and to me' (v.11).

Whenever someone comes to faith in Christ their whole life and outlook completely changes. Consequently, Onesimus realised the sin he had committed against the Lord and also the wrongs that had been done to Philemon. He was truly sorry and knew that it was essential to return and ask for forgiveness. This was a difficult challenge, for the offence was one of the most serious known to ancient law and the punishment could be brutal. Even so, there was no acceptable alternative. Being a Christian meant that he needed to make amends for his previous bad behaviour. Confessing you have been wrong is the first step to forgiveness.

On his return Onesimus would have been comforted by several factors. For example, there was the reassuring presence of a faithful Christian called Tychicus (Col. 4:7–9) and Paul's letter emphasising love and the spirit of forgiveness, which they were carrying with them. Philemon's reputation (vv.4–7), plus the past experience Onesimus had of his master, would give him hope. His new-found faith in Christ would also help him to conquer any fear.

As a man separated from Christ, it might have been impossible for Philemon to forgive Onesimus. However, being a Christian means that forgiveness should be a way of life (Matt. 18:21–22). Therefore, Paul can write confidently of Philemon's obedience to his request.

Discussion Starters

1. Satan leads people astray by making that which is bad appear to be good. Think of some biblical examples.

_____

_____

_____

_____

2. Onesimus ran away from a Christian environment. What do we learn from this?

_____

_____

_____

3. Why was it essential for Onesimus to return to the master he had wronged and seek forgiveness?

_____

_____

_____

4. What obstacles prevent us from asking for forgiveness from those we have wronged?

_____

_____

_____

5. How does the teaching of Jesus (Luke 15:11–32) relate to the experience of Onesimus?

_____

_____

_____

_____

6. Why is Paul confident that Philemon will forgive his slave?

_____

_____

_____

_____

7. How can we forgive those who have hurt us intensely?

_____

_____

_____

_____

8. Tychicus travelled with Onesimus to Colosse (Col. 4:7–9). Discuss the importance of fellowship between Christians of different doctrinal and social backgrounds.

_____

_____

_____

_____

Personal Application

Paul writes to Philemon, 'If [Onesimus] has done you any wrong or owes you anything, charge it to me' (v.18). He's offering to make restitution for Onesimus who has no way of repaying his debt. However, he also says, 'I, Paul, am writing this with my own hand. I will pay it back – not to mention that you owe me your very self' (v.19). I know Onesimus owes you a debt, but I remind you that your debt to me is greater. Therefore, put his debt on my account and then cancel it because you owe me considerably more.

Onesimus owes Philemon a material debt. Philemon owes Paul a spiritual debt. Paul had given him the gospel message and led him to the saving knowledge of Jesus Christ. How is he ever going to pay that back? How can we who owe a great eternal debt refuse to forgive the temporal debts of others?

Seeing Jesus in the Scriptures

For Jesus, forgiveness is central and occurs repeatedly throughout His ministry. He even forgave those who mocked and crucified Him: 'Father, forgive them, for they do not know what they are doing' (Luke 23:34). Because we acknowledge our own sinfulness, we are called to abundantly forgive those who sin against us (Col. 3:13). Jesus sets an example for us to follow.

WEEK 4

Thanksgiving and Prayer

Opening Icebreaker

Read together the Lord's prayer (Matt. 6:9–13). Observe that it begins with the glory of God, followed by the physical and spiritual needs of the person praying. This is the correct order for all our prayers.

Bible Readings

- Philemon 4–6; 22
- Colossians 4:2–4
- Romans 12:13
- 1 Peter 4:9

Opening Our Eyes

It is a serious mistake to believe that once you become a Christian all your problems will be solved. Quite the contrary! There is great danger in being a Christian within an unchristian society. Those who live a godly life in Christ Jesus will certainly be persecuted (2 Tim. 3:12).

Christians are saved from the penalty of sin, but not from suffering, as repeatedly illustrated in the life of Paul. Yet, despite his many trials, and whatever his circumstances, he thanked and praised God. For instance, when he and Silas were severely flogged and thrown into prison, they prayed and sang hymns to God (Acts 16:25). A feature of the Early Church was that they rejoiced because God had counted them worthy to suffer dishonour for the name of Jesus (Acts 5:41). Tertullian, the first great writer of Christian literature in Latin, rightly said, 'The legs feel nothing in the stocks when the heart is in heaven'.

In this letter to Philemon, the salutation (vv.1–3) is followed by thanksgiving and prayer. There is reference to love and joy because these are the fruit of faith. Paul was now a prisoner of the Roman authorities, but spiritually he was bound to the Lord Jesus Christ.

He writes to Philemon, 'I always thank my God as I remember you in my prayers' (v.4). Observe the words 'my God' – it is a personal relationship. This indicates that He is mine and I am His. Paul can express his thankfulness for the present problems are nothing compared to the glorious future which is secure in Christ.

Our gratitude to God will always be shown by our generosity to others. It's no wonder that Paul gives thanks for Philemon's love and kindness which had so often been an encouragement to God's people. To the

Ephesians Paul wrote, '... ever since I heard about your faith in the Lord Jesus and your love for all the saints, I have not stopped giving thanks for you, remembering you in my prayers' (Eph. 1:15–16). It is a tremendous joy and privilege to see a believer grow in their faith. For this one thanks God and prays that they will continue to spiritually mature.

Christian praise and prayer are inseparable. Prayer should begin with adoration and worship because of who God is. Christians should be constantly thankful for God's many blessings, but also conscious that so much more remains to be received. Consequently, Paul's spontaneous thanksgiving to God is immediately followed by a request for Philemon's needs. 'I pray that you may be active in sharing your faith, so that you will have a full understanding of every good thing we have in Christ' (v.6).

It is a prayer that Philemon, who had already been such a blessing in so many ways, may progress much further. The more he realises his debt to Christ, the more he will be inclined to show mercy to others, in this instance Onesimus. 'Bear with each other and forgive whatever grievances you may have against one another. Forgive as the Lord forgave you' (Col. 3:13).

Paul continues, 'Prepare a guest room for me, because I hope to be restored to you in answer to your prayers' (v.22). Hospitality and prayer are Christian duties, not optional extras. During his ministry, Paul constantly made appeals to be remembered in prayer (Rom. 15:30; Col. 4:3; 1 Thess. 5:25). Praise and prayer for oneself and others should be a fundamental characteristic of all Christians.

Discussion Starters

1. Why can those who live a godly life in Christ Jesus expect to be persecuted?

_____

_____

_____

_____

2. What do we learn from Paul's attitude to persecution?

_____

_____

_____

_____

3. How should we respond to suffering?

_____

_____

_____

_____

4. What are the elements of effective prayer?

_____

_____

_____

_____

5. Does God always answer prayer?

_____

_____

_____

_____

6. How important is worship to the life of a Christian?

_____

_____

_____

_____

7. If we are Christians, how should we behave towards one another (Luke 6:36; Eph. 5:1–2; Col. 3:13)?

_____

_____

_____

_____

8. Do all Christians need to practise hospitality, or does it apply to just a few (Isa. 58:7; Rom. 12:13; 1 Pet. 4:9)?

_____

_____

_____

_____

Personal Application

The subject of Paul's prayer (v.6) has caused translators extreme difficulty. Undoubtedly this is the most obscure verse in the whole letter. What are we to understand by the phrase 'be active in sharing your faith'? This appears to suggest telling others about Jesus Christ. However, Paul does not mean that in this instance. Sharing our faith indicates that we work together in Christ, rather than trying to go it alone.

Christian generosity was a conspicuous characteristic of Philemon; he had great love for God's people. Now Paul is asking him to be even more generous by showing mercy to the repentant Onesimus. Such faith expressing itself in love will lead one to a deeper trust in Christ. How does giving to others affect my own life?

Seeing Jesus in the Scriptures

None of the prayers of Jesus is recorded as fully as that found in John 17 where He prays for Himself, His disciples and for all believers. It has rightly been called His 'High Priestly Prayer' for He acts as the mediator between God the Father and humanity (Heb. 7:23–28).

The phrase 'The Lord's prayer' is a misnomer in that He Himself never prayed it. He could not say, 'Forgive us our sins, for we also forgive everyone who sins against us' (Luke 11:4). The first part would be inappropriate because although Jesus was a friend of sinners (Matt. 11:19), He was without sin.

WEEK 5

Paul's Appeal for Onesimus

Opening Icebreaker

Decisions influence our future for better or worse. What difficult decisions face Christians today? For example, how should we behave at work or conduct our social lives? Should we always stand firm in our faith even though it might prove to be unpopular? Suggest some principles of good decision making.

Bible Readings

- Philemon 8–25
- Proverbs 12:15
- Proverbs 13:14
- Proverbs 15:22

Opening Our Eyes

Paul boldly asks Philemon that Onesimus be forgiven. Even though conscious of his authority as an apostle of Christ, he does not demand it; rather he says that it is the right thing to do (v.8). He appeals to Philemon on the basis of Christian love. It is a request from a friend, an old man, now in prison for the sake of Christ Jesus.

Obviously Paul does not exclude any appeal to his authority, for if that were so he would not have referred to it at all. Similarly in verse 19 he says, '... not to mention that you owe me your very self'. Of course he *does* mention it! However, these are momentary persuasive thoughts for Philemon to consider, but they must not be the prime reason for his decision. He must be motivated by the teaching of God's Word that it is necessary to forgive those who have wronged us (Matt. 6:14–15). If the Lord has forgiven the slave, must he not be forgiven by his master?

No excuse is offered for Onesimus having run away. There is no denial of Philemon's right to punish his slave. Justice would demand that he did so. But there is a Christian plea for mercy from a fellow-worker. Surely, it would be impossible to refuse such a reasonable, though perhaps hard, request.

Because it was contrary to their nature, all of those involved faced a difficult decision. Paul was making a considerable sacrifice in telling Onesimus to return, and refers to him as 'my son' (v.10), and with him comes 'my very heart' (v.12). There is no doubt that Paul would have loved to keep him (v.13). Onesimus had to consider the possibility of severe punishment whilst Philemon had to receive back a slave who had been unreliable.

Despite the many difficulties, it was necessary for Onesimus to return and seek forgiveness. He had now become a Christian and so Paul tactfully suggests to Philemon the benefits of welcoming back this fugitive. Now he will be much more useful than before, both as a slave and as a brother in the Lord (v.16). They are now united in their allegiance to Christ. Paul argues that, 'Perhaps the reason he was separated from you for a little while was that you might have him back for good' (v.15). Through human disobedience Philemon lost a slave; but through Divine mercy, he gained a brother. Hopefully, Philemon would be able to treat him as if he were Paul himself.

If there is an outstanding debt because of theft, or any harm caused, Paul promises to be responsible for the restitution of former losses whatever the amount. Philemon, though, needs to remember his great debt to Paul, (v.19) and that there is an obligation to reciprocate. This is a principle which applies to both things received from God (v.6; Psa. 116:12) and from people (1 Tim. 5:4).

Although the letter is also addressed to Archippus, Apphia and the church, it is ultimately Philemon who must make the decision. Nevertheless, they can assist him to do his duty. Wise advisers are always to be welcomed for they can be the difference between success and failure. Will Philemon grant Paul's request? We are not told, but since in the past he has shown generosity to all believers, Paul is confident that he will do it again (v.21), this time to Onesimus.

Discussion Starters

1. What words does Paul use to describe his relationship with Onesimus (vv.10,12,16)? Consider what it cost Paul to send Onesimus back; and how joyfully he would have retained him.

_____

_____

_____

_____

2. Why does Paul request, rather than command, that Onesimus be forgiven?

_____

_____

_____

_____

3. Are our lives motivated by the teaching of God's Word?

_____

_____

_____

_____

4. Discuss how Christians are related to one another in the family of God.

_____

_____

_____

_____

5. What are the benefits of Christian love? How should it control our thoughts and actions?

_____

_____

_____

_____

6. Read Matthew 6:14–15 and discuss how it influences your way of thinking.

_____

_____

_____

_____

7. Paul writes, 'Perhaps the reason he was separated from you for a little while was that you might have him back for good' (v.15). What do you understand by this?

_____

_____

_____

_____

8. What is clear from this letter is that Paul is trying to involve the whole local church (v.2). Discuss the advantages of this.

_____

_____

_____

_____

Personal Application

It should be noted that what might appear to be a purely personal matter between two close friends is to be shared, not only with Apphia and Archippus, but also the church which met in Philemon's house. The expectation is that this letter would be read at a meeting of the house church. They need to hear what Paul would do in this difficult situation.

Should Onesimus be forgiven? Though ultimately Philemon must decide whether Paul's request will be granted, the others must influence and advise him to do his duty. All true Christians belong to the family of God and Onesimus is now one of them. Hence, the action taken will affect the whole Church. 'If one part suffers, every part suffers with it; if one part is honoured, every part rejoices with it' (1 Cor. 12:26). Sharing is a clear expression of our love.

Seeing Jesus in the Scriptures

Jesus answered Thomas, 'I am the way and the truth and the life. No-one comes to the Father except through me' (John 14:6). It was Jesus' decision to voluntarily sacrifice His life as a ransom for many (Matt. 20:28) so that everyone who believes in Him will not perish (John 3:16). The most important decision anyone can make is to follow God and believe in His only begotten Son. A failure to do so will result in being condemned to hell.

WEEK 6

Slaves and Masters

Opening Icebreaker

Discuss the reasons why God allows challenges in our lives, personal and more far-reaching, such as dealing with issues of social injustice. How does He enable us to face such challenges?

Bible Readings

- Philemon 12–16
- Colossians 3:22 – 4:1
- 1 Timothy 6:1–2
- Titus 2:9–10
- 1 Corinthians 7:21–24

Opening Our Eyes

Slavery, whereby one person owns another as a piece of property, was a common and widespread practice in Bible times. The Old Testament says that an Israelite who sold himself to pay a debt must be set free after a period of six years (Exod. 21:2), or sooner if it was the Jubilee year (Lev. 25:39–41). An Israelite could sell his capacity for work, but not his body and so rather than a slave, he was a hired worker. Upon his release, he was to be liberally provided for (Deut. 15:13–15).

It was different for non-Israelites; they could be forever slaves if payment was not made for their release. However, it should be remembered that in Israel, slaves were never regarded only as property. Regulations under Israelite law protected them as human beings. Male slaves were to be circumcised like any Israelite male (Gen. 17:12–13) and were to share in religious celebrations such as the Passover (Exod. 12:44). Hebrew slavery was less severe than Greek practice; and Greek than Roman.

Slavery in the Greek and Roman world of the New Testament was an indispensable part of the social system and accounted for a large percentage of the population. Slaves might be inherited, purchased or acquired, either in settlement of a bad debt or as a prisoner of war. They had no rights of their own and were sometimes treated like chattels. The Greek philosopher Aristotle said, 'A slave is a living tool', which indicates dehumanisation and exploitation. Roman law permitted owners to discipline their slaves as they wished. Hence, cruelty was a frequent occurrence, even to the extreme of having them thrown to wild beasts or crucified for the most trivial offence.

Despite this, it would be wrong to assume that such treatment was universal. Many were well treated and certainly some early Christians owned slaves as the letter to

Philemon makes clear. Even so, irrespective of the varying degrees of degradation, one cannot ever condone slavery.

Eventually this evil practice became outlawed in civilised countries through the efforts of men like William Wilberforce who, following his conversion to evangelical Christianity, was prominent in the struggle to abolish slavery. Why didn't Paul advocate the instant, absolute emancipation of slaves? Did he feel powerless to act?

Revolution of love

Undoubtedly a rebellion would have resulted in a massacre and created far more problems than it solved. This approach was definitely not the answer. Rather, Paul looked at the social system and endeavoured by peaceful means to abolish slavery. He tactfully says, 'Slaves, obey your earthly masters with respect and fear, and with sincerity of heart, just as you would obey Christ ... And masters, treat your slaves in the same way' (Eph. 6:5–9). It is love that enables one to show love and compassion to others. 'I love my master and my wife and children and do not want to go free' (Exod. 21:5) would be complemented by the attitude of the centurion towards his servant (Luke 7:1–9). Such attitudes abolish slavery; for to treat people with love means that they are no longer a piece of property but a person. It creates a new relationship between slave and master. This was the correct and only long-term solution and is equally applicable in solving the many social injustices encountered today. The truth of the gospel, for example Matthew 5:43–48; Romans 12:9–14 and 1 Corinthians 13, will achieve infinitely more than physical violence.

Discussion Starters

1. Does Philemon help us to understand how employers should treat their employees?

_____

_____

_____

_____

2. How should employees respond to their employers? Why?

_____

_____

_____

_____

3. Should Paul's response have been to call for the immediate abolition of slavery? Should Christians call for its immediate abolition today?

_____

_____

_____

_____

4. Returning a runaway slave to his master to become enslaved once more is strictly forbidden (Deut. 23:15). Was Paul wrong in sending Onesimus back?

_____

_____

_____

_____

5. What does Paul's attitude to slavery and social injustice teach us today? For example: if we were living under a dictatorship or working for an oppressive employer.

_____

_____

_____

_____

6. People who are oppressed can often be used mightily in God's service. Think of some biblical examples.

_____

_____

_____

_____

7. Why is it wrong to compare oneself with other people?

_____

_____

_____

_____

8. In what practical ways can Christians influence society? Does the Church influence our nation today?

_____

_____

_____

_____

Personal Application

The New Testament writers never directly suggest the abolition of slavery, but they do lay down rules of behaviour for Christian masters. Even though Paul does not condemn the institution of slavery, he is sowing the seeds of emancipation. Obviously, if the principle of loving your neighbour as yourself (Matt. 19:19) were carried to fruition, slavery would be constrained and eventually abolished.

Christians differ greatly from one another in social standing, culture, temperament and in numerous other ways. Thank God we do. These differences should never prevent fellowship because our shared partnership in Christ makes all class distinction totally irrelevant (Rom. 12:5). Do we readily accept each other as equals, brothers and sisters in Christ?

Seeing Jesus in the Scriptures

Jesus frequently angered His opponents by crossing widely accepted boundaries. He mixed with people they did not like (Mark 2:16). Surely, sinners should not be associated with by the so-called righteous? These unsympathetic critics failed to realise that Jesus, by associating with such outcasts, was meeting a vital need. Healthy people do not need a doctor – sick people do. Jesus did not come to call those who thought themselves good enough – but sinners.

As Jesus crosses many boundaries, a new boundary is drawn. People are divided into those who respond to His message and those who reject it. Ultimately these are the only two categories of people in the world. 'There is neither Jew nor Greek, slave nor free, male nor female, for you are all one in Christ Jesus' (Gal. 3:28).

WEEK 7

Concluding Thoughts

Opening Icebreaker

The theme of forgiveness is prominent in Jesus' ministry. Discuss: What does it really mean to be forgiven? Must I forgive those who have hurt me deeply and what are the consequences of withholding forgiveness?

Bible Readings

- Philemon 8–21
- Romans 3:9–20
- Philippians 2:1–11
- 1 John 1:8–10

Opening Our Eyes

Paul's letter to Philemon reveals the pattern of Christianity. Firstly, there is a picture of sin. When God made us it was for the purpose of serving Him; but there is no one who does what is right (Psa. 14:3; Rom. 3:10–11). All have broken away from God to live for self. What is sin? Very simply, it is to be a runaway slave.

The punishment of slaves was much harsher and more humiliating than that of free people. Roman law permitted a master to treat them however he liked. Consequently, runaways or thieves, if caught, would often face brutal punishment. Being condemned to hard labour, chained up, severe lashing and many other forms of barbarism were common. A slave who stole might be branded by their master on the face with the letters CF, representing the words *Cave furem* meaning 'Beware the thief'. By far the worst punishment was death by crucifixion, for this intentionally delayed death until the maximum pain had been inflicted. Not until Constantine the Great (AD 306–337), the first Roman emperor to profess to be a Christian, were crucifixion and branding of the face as punishments banned. Even so, slaves could still be severely punished.

In the Bible, there is only one punishment for sin and that is death, but the gift of God is eternal life in Christ Jesus our Lord (Rom. 6:23).

Paul uses powerful arguments (especially v.19) in his heart-rending appeal on behalf of Onesimus. He will pay the debt whatever the sacrifice so as to promote perfect Christian fellowship. God has paid the price of our sins 'not with perishable things such as silver or gold … but with the precious blood of Christ, a lamb without blemish or defect' (1 Pet. 1:18–19). And in Jesus not only do we have someone to pay our debt, but someone to plead for us (Rom. 8:34).

Paul's behaviour displays the love of Jesus which should be a characteristic of all Christians. What God is to us, we must be towards others. Only then will there be a flow of God's forgiving love permeating a sinful world.

Reading this letter, one observes a picture of salvation, of justification and sanctification. Justification takes place only once in our lives and can simply be described as a change of status whereby we are declared righteous. On the other hand, sanctification is a continuous renewal of the heart which is never completed in this life and results in a change of character. 'God the Father declares the sinner righteous, and God the Holy Spirit sanctifies him.'[1] With Onesimus, the change of status is from a slave into a son and likewise those who are saved by grace and through faith in Christ become sons (Heb. 12:6–7). Onesimus' change of character is that from being useless he became useful.

A personal relationship with Christ leads to a new way of life. Paul says, 'I have been crucified with Christ and I no longer live, but Christ lives in me' (Gal. 2:20). Conversion involves a change of slavery, from being slaves to sin to slaves of righteousness (Rom. 6:17–18). Christians should be living witnesses of Christ wherever they go.

Paul, Philemon and Onesimus are very diverse characters and yet all are Christians. All were equal before God, for Christ is all, and is in all (Col. 3:11).

---

1. L. Berkhof, *Systematic Theology* (Edinburgh: Banner of Truth, 1974) p.514.

Discussion Starters

1. What is sin and how will it be punished?

2. Discuss what you understand by the word 'justification'. Why does it lie at the very heart of Christianity?

3. Why is justification by works of the law impossible?

4. What do you understand by the word 'sanctification'? How does this differ from justification?

5. Should Christians welcome back into fellowship those who have committed crimes or serious sins?

6. Discuss what social barriers exist today. How does Jesus break down these barriers?

7. What do you know about Epaphras, Mark, Aristarchus, Demas and Luke (Philem. vv.23–24)?

8. As we come to a conclusion of our study, what significant lessons have you learnt from this short letter?

Personal Application

God calls not only for a change of heart but also a change of behaviour. Our Christian beliefs should always affect our actions. This does not mean that we will not sin again; we will. But as long as we are living close to God, we desire to show our faith by our actions and make amends to any we might have wronged.

The conversion of Zacchaeus clearly illustrates this principle. He was considered by his fellow countrypeople to be a notorious sinner because he collected taxes for the Romans. Hence, many were displeased when Jesus said, 'I must stay in your house today' (Luke 19:5). Barriers were broken and Zacchaeus realised the great love God had for him. He responded by giving to the poor and promised to pay back four times the amount owed to any he had cheated.

Does this apply to you?

Seeing Jesus in the Scriptures

Jesus says to Thomas, 'I am the way and the truth and the life. No-one comes to the Father except through me' (John 14:6). This summarises all His work and teaching. He is the only mediator between God and humanity. Therefore, though conversion experiences happen in many different ways, they have one common factor. Change only comes as the result of a personal encounter with Jesus Christ. 'If anyone is in Christ, he is a new creation; the old has gone, the new has come!' (2 Cor. 5:17) Do you accept this to be true?

Leader's Notes

Week 1: Paul, a Prisoner of Christ Jesus

Icebreaker
The idea of this exercise is for the group to consider what it means to be Christ-like so as to produce abundant spiritual fruit (Gal. 5:22–23).

Aim of the Session
To show that the Holy Spirit, working within Paul, changes him to become more and more like Jesus. Can people see a living and active faith in our lives?

Discussion Starters
1. Truth is often distorted to create an ideology that incites intolerance. 'You are free to believe whatever you want – providing it is the same as me.' Tragically, many monstrous acts have been committed in the name of Christ. Examples are the Christian Crusades, the Inquisition and those who suffered martyrdom during the reign of Queen Mary I because of their beliefs. Paul was a persecutor of Christians, because formerly he was convinced that they were blasphemers. You can be sincere, but wrong.

2. Paul believed in doctrine (for his message was based on theology), but not in indoctrination. He did not expect what was taught to be accepted without examination of the Scriptures. In comparison, indoctrination is to teach someone to accept uncritically what are often partisan or tendentious ideas. Discernment based on God's Word is essential for training in righteousness (2 Tim. 3:16–17).

3. The opposition of the Pharisees against Jesus was primarily due to the fact that He called Himself the Son

of God. This they could not tolerate (Matt. 26:63–65). Saul was a well-educated, strict Pharisee who truly believed that his persecution of Christians was the will of God. He was wrong. Eagerness, earnestness, enthusiasm and popularity are not always indicative that something is true (1 Kings 18:25–29).

4. Saul savagely opposed Christians because he was convinced that they were heretics and a serious threat to Judaism. He could boast, 'I was advancing in Judaism beyond many Jews of my own age and was extremely zealous for the traditions of my fathers' (Gal. 1:14). He had been influenced by human traditions rather than God's holy law. Controlling our emotions by the power of the Holy Spirit is a characteristic of spiritual maturity.

5. Saul's violent opposition to Christianity clearly reveals that he did not choose Christ, but that Christ chose him. The Lord said to Ananias, 'This man is my chosen instrument ...' (Acts 9:15). The conversion of Saul clearly reveals God's sovereignty in the process of salvation and how the Holy Spirit can penetrate the most hardened heart. Therefore, we should never despair for those who are opposed to the gospel message.

6. God does not show partiality and neither should we (Deut. 10:17; Acts 10:34–35).
Consider the following examples of prejudice:

- Race (John 4:9; Acts 10:28)
- Wealth (Prov. 14:20–21; James 2:1–9)
- Appearance (1 Sam. 16:7)
- Age (1 Tim. 4:12)
- Occupation (Mark 6:2–3)

The world hates all those who believe in Jesus and so Christians will inevitably experience prejudice (John 15:19).

7. A tactful person is not one who avoids difficult situations. He or she will admonish or rebuke where necessary. However, one does have an intuitive perception of the right thing to do or say. There are numerous examples of this within the Bible such as: Nathan's story of the 'little ewe lamb' (2 Sam. 12:1–12); Joseph's attitude to Mary (Matt. 1:19) and Gamaliel's advice to the Sanhedrin (Acts 5:33–40).

8. Paul identifies himself not as a prisoner of Rome but of Jesus Christ. He was in prison because Christ put him there. Despite imprisonment, God still used him. Consider similar situations that exist today. Examples would be those who are housebound due to age or illness. Remember that God can use us in any circumstances.

Week 2: Philemon, a Fellow-Worker

Icebreaker
The aim of this exercise is to see how we can help others both spiritually and physically. Often just a smile can be a tremendous encouragement.

Aim of the Session
To consider the supremacy of Christ and the many dangers of being perverted by wrong teaching.

Discussion Starters
1. Paul thanked God for the Colossian Christians because of their faith in Christ Jesus and the love they had for all believers. This faith and love is due to the fact that they were confidently looking forward to the joys of heaven (Col. 1:3–8).

2. Paul confronts the false teaching endangering the church at Colosse (Col. 2:6–23). Discuss these problems

and consider how they apply to us in the twenty-first century. Religious observances and rules are always dangerous if we believe they can achieve more than Christ can give us.

3. In Colossians 1:7 we see that Paul calls Epaphras his 'dear fellow-servant, who is a faithful minister of Christ'. He was always wrestling in prayer and working hard for those who believed, that they might mature and be confident in the will of God (Col. 4:12–13). Epaphras is not a well-known figure in history but he was faithful to the Lord, and that is the only vital thing in any person's life. He was Paul's fellow-prisoner in Christ Jesus (Philem. 23). Certainly Epaphras was a man to be imitated.

4. Do we boast of anything except Christ? Let us learn from Paul (Col. 1:15–23) that to trust in anything except the supremacy of Christ is a mistake and does not lead to heaven. Hence, it is vital at all times to give Christ the central place; otherwise you lose direction and eventually disintegrate and die: '... no-one can lay any foundation other than the one already laid, which is Jesus Christ' (1 Cor. 3:11). This is the only true foundation on which the Church is built for Christ will not share His glory with anything or anyone else.

5. Philemon had a true reputation for trusting in the Lord Jesus which resulted in a love for all believers. He was generous because of his faith. Observe (v.5) that he had a love for all believers irrespective of their background or present state. His kindness so often refreshed the hearts of God's people.

6. Does faith in Christ mean that we can live as we please? No. Faith, if it is not accompanied by action, is dead and therefore useless (James 2:17). A genuine faith in Christ Jesus will express itself visibly through love (Gal. 5:6). Can our friends and neighbours see the

evidence of a living and active faith within us?

7. Money itself is not evil (1 Tim. 6:10) and can be enjoyed and used to God's glory. It is the *love* of money which is the problem. Those who are avaricious will show little, if any, concern for the poor. All our resources come from God and should be generously used in ways that honour Him and help others. Jesus said, 'You cannot serve both God and Money' (Luke 16:13).

8. Philemon employed slave labour at a time when slavery was common. Slaves constituted the workforce of the Roman Empire and this was not considered to be a problem. Even so, it is impossible to defend slavery in God's name. When Christian masters regarded slaves as brothers and sisters instead of property, the bondage would no longer exist. That is what happened as the Spirit of Christ worked in people's lives.

Week 3: Onesimus, a Runaway Slave

Icebreaker
Consider organisations such as Fairtrade (www.fairtrade. org.uk) which help to ensure that disadvantaged producers in the developing world receive a fair price for their produce. Would members of the group be prepared to pay extra so that retailers will support such schemes?

Aim of the Session
To show that it is important to confess sin to those whom you have wronged, and that the spirit of forgiveness should know no boundaries.

Discussion Starters
1. Biblical examples include the temptation of Eve (Gen. 3); observe in verse 6 that the fruit was 'pleasing

to the eye'. Also look at the temptation of Jesus
(Matt. 4:1–11). Emphasise that temptation is conquered by
using 'the sword of the Spirit, which is the word of God'
(Eph. 6:17).

2. It would be a mistake to believe that the environment
always influences our behaviour. Onesimus running away,
or problems within Christian families today, should not
surprise us. Why? Because it was in paradise, the perfect
environment, that Adam and Eve sinned.

3. Onesimus had run away. Hence, he must go back
and face up to the consequences of what he had done.
Confessing his error was the first step to forgiveness.
Similarly Christianity does not enable us to run away
from our past; rather it helps us to rise above it. Making
restitution where necessary is evidence of a changed life.

4. To seek forgiveness, there must first be a realisation
that you have done wrong. Proud behaviour can result in
our inability to accept or see the truth. The other extreme
is to believe that our sin is so great that it cannot be
forgiven. Feelings of shame must never prevent us from
saying sorry (see 1 John 1:9).

5. The younger son (Luke 15:11–32) was tired of staying
at home; typical of some people today. He wanted to be
free of all authority and interference. Before leaving home,
he would have been wise to ask himself how long this
so-called freedom would last and what would be the end
result. He learnt the answers to these questions in the
school of experience and endured great suffering prior to
realising his foolishness and returning home. Get the group
to identify the similarities between this son and Onesimus.

6. Paul expresses his thanks for the virtues which have
characterised Philemon in the past, especially his love
for all God's people. It is because of Philemon's past

performance (vv.4–7) that Paul is confident his plea will faithfully be carried out and more besides (v.21). Probably Philemon did not disappoint, since this letter has survived. He didn't tear it up!

7. Corrie ten Boom spent part of World War 2 in a Nazi concentration camp and suffered horrendously. After the war she travelled extensively, speaking about the love and forgiveness of God. In her book *Tramp for the Lord* (Corrie ten Boom with Jamie Buckingham, London: Hodder & Stoughton, 1974), she recalls speaking at a church in Munich and being approached by one of her cruellest former camp guards who had since become a Christian. It was not easy to forgive, but she did. For a long moment they grasped each other's hands.

8. For some, fellowship means no more than meeting together for church events. This is wrong. Biblical fellowship involves a serious commitment based on mutual love. Fellowship was a powerful witness of the Early Church (Acts 4:32–37). True Christian fellowship can only be achieved by submission to the authority of the Holy Spirit who will never lead believers into disunity, despite their differing peripheral doctrinal beliefs or background.

Week 4: Thanksgiving and Prayer

Icebreaker
Allow group members the opportunity to add their own prayers after the Lord's prayer.

Aim of the Session
To show that thanksgiving and prayer are at the heart of the Christian faith even during times of adversity.

Discussion Starters

1. The aim of the Christian life should be to imitate Christ's likeness. Consequently, this will lead to persecution because the godly always arouse the antagonism of the worldly. It has always been so. It was so for Christ, and He said that we could expect the same (John 15:18–20). Paul's experience of severe suffering is not unique. Everyone who becomes increasingly like Christ will be treated increasingly like Him.

2. Paul was convinced that the sufferings of this present life, painful though they are (as he well knew from experience), are not worthy to be compared to the future glory (Rom. 8:18). Writing to the Corinthians he said, '… our light and momentary troubles are achieving for us an eternal glory that far outweighs them all' (2 Cor. 4:17). Observe the opposites: momentary – eternal, troubles – glory. Paul's faith triumphed over affliction because he looked to the future. He cast his eyes upon Jesus.

3. Does suffering make us bitter or better? If bad things happen to us can we say with Job, 'The LORD gave and the LORD has taken away; may the name of the LORD be praised' (Job 1:21)? Trials are the means God uses to strengthen and mature us.

4. A disciple asked Jesus to teach them how to pray (Luke 11:1). He responded with what we call the Lord's prayer. This, through an economy of words, thus avoiding meaningless verbosity (Matt. 6:7–8), reveals the basic pattern of effective prayer. This is adoration, confession and dedication as well as requests. This prayer may be used literally as a fixed liturgical prayer, or each phrase may be expanded into a wider range of expressions.

5. Sometimes, like Paul, we discover that God does not always give us what we ask for (2 Cor. 12:7–10). Rather He provides what is essential for our spiritual well-being.

Hence, the answer to a sincere prayer may be yes, no, or wait. All true prayer is based on the theme 'your will be done' (Matt. 6:10). Even Jesus submits to the will of His Father (Matt. 26:39).

6. The noun 'worship' is a contraction of 'worthship'. Therefore, to worship God is to acknowledge His worth or worthiness. It is to recognise who God is (Rev. 17:14) and thank Him for His abundant blessings. Our worship of God is a foretaste of heaven.

7. We should imitate Jesus Christ in serving others and so treat them with compassion, kindness, humility, gentleness, patience and love. It is necessary to love one another as God has loved us. Love is willing to sacrifice for the benefit of others, even to death. If ever we are to become great we must be prepared to become slaves and servants of others.

8. Hospitality is a prominent feature of the Early Church. They met in houses, not church buildings, and frequently shared meals together. Paul considers the virtue of hospitality so important that he makes it a requirement for anyone who desires to be an overseer in the Church (1 Tim. 3:2) and 1 Peter 4:9 broadens this to include all of us. The aim is not to impress people; it is about making them feel wanted and welcome.

Week 5: Paul's Appeal for Onesimus

Icebreaker
The idea of this exercise is for the group to identify difficult decisions facing Christians today. Our decisions must never contradict God's Word.

Aim of the Session

To consider how we face decisions that may affect the rest of our lives.

Discussion Starters

1. Paul calls Onesimus 'my son' (v.10); 'my very heart' (v.12) and 'very dear' (v.16). Observe Paul's intense depth of feeling for this newly-won convert to the Christian faith.

2. If Paul had commanded Philemon to forgive Onesimus, it would not have been an independent decision. It may have been done grudgingly rather than gladly, with the consequence that love which is very forgetful when it comes to remembering injury and injustice will be absent. Onesimus would have been physically free, but Philemon would become a spiritual slave; something far worse than being a physical slave. Philemon must be motivated by the clear teaching of God's Word, and love Onesimus as a dear brother.

3. God has given us the Bible so that we can understand life and the principles of life. It teaches us what is true and enables us to realise what is wrong in our lives (2 Tim. 3:16). The more we know God's Word, the better able we shall be to deal with life's many problems. Let us always be careful to avoid placing our own word or thoughts over the authority of the Word of God. Mature Christian discipleship is impossible if we are not prepared to submit fully to our Lord's teaching authority as it is mediated through Scripture.

4. Christianity is all about a relationship (Gal. 3:26). Those who know Jesus Christ as their Lord and Saviour are adopted into God's family. He becomes their Father and they become His children. Therefore, this means that all Christians, despite their cultural backgrounds and denominational differences, are brothers and sisters. Being a Christian is to enter into a real family relationship.

5. Philemon had a reputation for love which gave Paul great joy and encouragement. Anyone who loves the Lord Jesus Christ, anyone who loves their fellow Christians, is going to show their love by being a forgiver. Love is patient and kind and does not keep a record of wrongs. A refusal to forgive produces bitterness.

6. Our eagerness to forgive the sins of others reveals that we are children of God and that we have had our own sins forgiven. Consequently, for a Christian, a failure to forgive is unthinkable. However, this does raise the vital question, 'Does not the offender also have an obligation?' The answer is 'Yes', it is necessary to show repentance (Luke 17:3–4). Onesimus was repentant and so Philemon had a duty to forgive. Do law suits against almost everyone and everything, conceivable and inconceivable, suggest that Christianity does not restrain society to the extent that it once did?

7. Paul contrasts the short period of Onesimus' deliberate absence with the eventual outcome. He does not condone what had happened, but tentatively suggests that Philemon carefully considers God's overruling providence in this situation. The temporary loss became an eternal gain.

8. This letter is intended primarily for Philemon, but his response to Onesimus will undoubtedly also affect Apphia, Archippus and the church that met in his house. Therefore, although Philemon must take the final decision, the church, too, must hear what Paul says. Then they will be able to assist Philemon to do his duty and accept Onesimus into the fellowship as a dear brother in the Lord. Onesimus has done his part; he is repentant and now it is the turn of Philemon.

Week 6: Slaves and Masters

Icebreaker

To show that challenges are opportunities to grow spiritually, to become more Christ-like (James 1:2–4). We should not be discouraged by the size of the challenge – even 'big issues' such as social injustice – but rather encouraged by the power of God (1 Sam. 17:41–47). The problems ahead of us are never as great as the power behind us.

Aim of the Session

To show that love for our neighbour abolishes slavery and social injustice.

Discussion Starters

1. God is no respecter of persons (Col. 3:25). Therefore, masters as well as slaves will be judged and rewarded or punished according to their actions. 'Masters, provide your slaves with what is right and fair, because you know that you also have a Master in heaven' (Col. 4:1). These principles are still relevant to Christian employers and employees. Their ultimate aim in all things should be the glory of God, whatever the cost.

2. 'Slaves, obey your earthly masters in everything' (Col. 3:22). This should be done willingly, '… so that in every way they will make the teaching about God our Saviour attractive' (Titus 2:10). The primary concern for Christians should be to lead their employers to salvation, thus making them members of God's family. All Christians should ensure that their lifestyle is beyond reproach, putting into practice what they preach.

3. Slavery was deeply rooted in Roman society and to call for its abolition is something the Christian communities of the first century were in no position to do. Any social revolution would have been immediately crushed by the

authorities and also many a slave was totally dependent on their master for survival. It is not surprising therefore, that Paul advocates a policy of non-violence. We must not let evil defeat us (Rom. 12:17–21). Many people who enjoy freedom today might still be slaves if not for Christ's influence on the world.

4. The person referred to in Deuteronomy 23:15 was probably a foreign refugee who must not be exploited, extradited or sold again into slavery. Israel was to be a place of safety for those who had been abused by their masters. Hagar was told to return to her mistress (Gen. 16:9). Paul sent Onesimus back to his master because he was confident that he would be received as a brother in the Lord.

5. Paul did not support slavery. He spoke of 'slave traders' as 'ungodly and sinful' (1 Tim. 1:9–10). He told slaves, 'if you can gain your freedom, do so' (1 Cor. 7:21). Although speaking up for the poor and helpless, he was humble, patient and kind. His way to abolish slavery was to sow quietly the seeds of emancipation by preaching the gospel of Jesus Christ. This is the way to bridge the many problems that divide society today.

6. Biblical examples you could look at of those who served God whilst oppressed are: Joseph in Egypt, Esther in Persia, Daniel in Babylon and Paul in prison.

7. Comparing yourself to other people is sinful. A feeling of superiority results in pride, whilst inferiority leads to envy. Our shared partnership in Christ makes any class distinction irrelevant.

8. Throughout history, Christians have spoken out against injustice and have often been instrumental in changing the laws of the land. Lord Shaftesbury campaigned against vile conditions in factories and the lack of education for poor children. Archbishop Desmond Tutu was awarded the

Nobel Peace Prize because of his quest for a non-violent end to apartheid in South Africa. Likewise, Christians today must strive to achieve standards that are in accordance with God's will. Does the Church influence our nation today? To what extent does the nation influence the Church?

Week 7: Concluding Thoughts

Opening Icebreaker

The idea of this exercise is to stress that we are to forgive because our Father in heaven has forgiven us. If we refuse to forgive others who repent, we forfeit our fellowship with God.

Aim of the Session

To show that the book of Philemon teaches us that God changes lives.

Discussion Starters

1. 'Everyone who sins breaks the law; in fact sin is lawlessness' (1 John 3:4). The standard against which sin is to be judged is the law of God. All have sinned (Rom. 3:19,23), and the wages of sin is death (Rom. 6:23), but God gives us what we do not deserve, the gift of eternal life. The only condition of receiving this is that we are personally united to our Lord Jesus Christ by faith.

2. Paul in his letter to the Galatians (2:16–21) reveals the doctrine of justification by faith. This doctrine lies at the heart of Christianity and so it is vital that we understand it. Justification is the opposite of condemnation (Rom. 8:1,33). To justify is to declare someone innocent or righteous. In the Bible it refers to God's act of grace (undeserved favour) by which He pardons our sins and accepts us as righteous in His sight.

3. If anyone could have been saved by strict adherence to the law, Paul would have been a strong contender (Phil. 3:4–6). His outward appearance was irreproachable. However, through the law he had discovered what a great sinner he was (Rom. 3:20). Only by the act of justification does God radically change our legal standing before His law (Rom. 5:1).

4. Sanctification is a transformation into God's likeness (2 Cor. 3:17–18), by the power of the Holy Spirit (2 Thess. 2:13). Whilst justification occurs only once in your life; sanctification is a gradual and progressive lifelong process of growing in holiness and becoming Christ-like.

5. It is probably difficult for Philemon to regard a runaway slave as a brother, but that is what Paul requests. 'So if you consider me a partner, welcome him as you would welcome me' (v.17). Christians should always welcome back into fellowship those who have made a serious error, providing they show remorse. Sometimes we may believe that God can forgive them; but that we are not able. Remember that our Lord taught us to pray, 'Forgive us our sins, for we also forgive everyone who sins against us' (Luke 11:4).

6. All people are not born equal. Numerous barriers exist between classes, cultures, races and religious beliefs. Even amongst Christians, denominational differences can cause major problems. We need to remember that God has united all believers in Christ Jesus and that all are equal (Gal. 3:28; Col. 3:11). We are equal in our need of salvation, equal in our inability to earn it, and equal in that God offers it to us freely in Christ.

7. *Epaphras*: probably the founder of the church at Colosse. Now a fellow prisoner with Paul.

Mark: or John Mark (Acts 12:12,25) accompanied Paul on his first missionary journey. They later parted company (Acts 13:13; 15:37–39). Now working together again.

Aristarchus: formerly came from Thessalonica (Acts 20:4). Later accompanied Paul on his journey from Jerusalem to Rome (Acts 27:2).

Demas: a fellow-worker. He eventually deserted the cause (2 Tim. 4:10).

Luke: wrote the third Gospel and the book of Acts. He was in Rome during Paul's first Roman imprisonment (Col. 4:14) and his second (2 Tim. 4:11).

8. Give everyone the opportunity to ask questions they still have about the letter to Philemon. Try to answer these together. If necessary, seek help from your church leaders. What have you learnt from your studies? What were the most important truths you discovered about Paul, Philemon, Onesimus and yourself? How will this influence the way you live?

National Distributors

UK: (and countries not listed below)
CWR, Waverley Abbey House, Waverley Lane, Farnham, Surrey GU9 8EP. Tel: (01252) 784700
Outside UK (44) 1252 784700 Email: mail@cwr.org.uk

AUSTRALIA: KI Entertainment, Unit 21 317-321 Woodpark Road, Smithfield, New South Wales 2164.
Tel: 1 800 850 777 Fax: 02 9604 3699 Email: sales@kientertainment.com.au

CANADA: David C Cook Distribution Canada, PO Box 98, 55 Woodslee Avenue, Paris, Ontario
N3L 3E5. Tel: 1800 263 2664 Email: sandi.swanson@davidccook.ca

GHANA: Challenge Enterprises of Ghana, PO Box 5723, Accra. Tel: (021) 222437/223249
Fax: (021) 226227 Email: ceg@africaonline.com.gh

HONG KONG: Cross Communications Ltd, 1/F, 562A Nathan Road, Kowloon. Tel: 2780 1188
Fax: 2770 6229 Email: cross@crosshk.com

INDIA: Crystal Communications, 10-3-18/4/1, East Marredpalli, Secunderabad – 500026, Andhra
Pradesh. Tel/Fax: (040) 27737145 Email: crystal_edwj@rediffmail.com

KENYA: Keswick Books and Gifts Ltd, PO Box 10242-00400, Nairobi. Tel: (254) 20 312639/3870125
Email: keswick@swiftkenya.com

MALAYSIA: Canaanland, No. 25 Jalan PJU 1A/41B, NZX Commercial Centre, Ara Jaya, 47301 Petaling
Jaya, Selangor. Tel: (03) 7885 0540/1/2 Fax: (03) 7885 0545 Email: info@canaanland.com.my

Salvation Book Centre (M) Sdn Bhd, 23 Jalan SS 2/64, 47300 Petaling Jaya, Selangor.
Tel: (03) 78766411/78766797 Fax: (03) 78757066/78756360 Email: info@salvationbookcentre.com

NEW ZEALAND: KI Entertainment, Unit 21 317-321 Woodpark Road, Smithfield, New South Wales
2164, Australia. Tel: 0 800 850 777 Fax: +612 9604 3699 Email: sales@kientertainment.com.au

NIGERIA: FBFM, Helen Baugh House, 96 St Finbarr's College Road, Akoka, Lagos.
Tel: (01) 7747429/4700218/825775/827264 Email: fbfm_1@yahoo.com

PHILIPPINES: OMF Literature Inc, 776 Boni Avenue, Mandaluyong City. Tel: (02) 531 2183
Fax: (02) 531 1960 Email: gloadlaon@omflit.com

SINGAPORE: Alby Commercial Enterprises Pte Ltd, 95 Kallang Avenue #04–00, AIS Industrial
Building, 339420. Tel: (65) 629 27238 Fax: (65) 629 27235 Email: marketing@alby.com.sg

SOUTH AFRICA: Struik Christian Books, 80 MacKenzie Street, PO Box 1144, Cape Town 8000.
Tel: (021) 462 4360 Fax: (021) 461 3612 Email: info@struikchristianmedia.co.za

SRI LANKA: Christombu Publications (Pvt) Ltd, Bartleet House, 65 Braybrooke Place, Colombo 2.
Tel: (9411) 2421073/2447665 Email: dhanad@bartleet.com

USA: David C Cook Distribution Canada, PO Box 98, 55 Woodslee Avenue, Paris, Ontario N3L 3E5,
Canada. Tel: 1800 263 2664 Email: sandi.swanson@davidccook.ca

CWR is a Registered Charity - Number 294387
CWR is a Limited Company registered in England - Registration Number 1990308

Courses and seminars

Publishing and new media

Conference facilities

Transforming lives

CWR's vision is to enable people to experience personal transformation through applying God's Word to their lives and relationships.

Our Bible-based training and resources help people around the world to:
• Grow in their walk with God
• Understand and apply Scripture to their lives
• Resource themselves and their church
• Develop pastoral care and counselling skills
• Train for leadership
• Strengthen relationships, marriage and family life and much more.

Our insightful writers provide daily Bible-reading notes and other resources for all ages, and our experienced course designers and presenters have gained an international reputation for excellence and effectiveness.

CWR's Training and Conference Centre in Surrey, England, provides excellent facilities in an idyllic setting – ideal for both learning and spiritual refreshment.

Applying God's Word
to everyday life and relationships

CWR, Waverley Abbey House,
Waverley Lane, Farnham,
Surrey GU9 8EP, UK

Telephone: **+44 (0)1252 784700**
Email: **info@cwr.org.uk**
Website: **www.cwr.org.uk**

Registered Charity No 294387
Company Registration No 1990308

Dramatic new resources

The Ten Commandments – Living God's Way
by Mary Evans

See the Ten Commandments in their original context and discover what they can mean for us today. But be warned: thoughtful study of this topic can be life changing!
ISBN: 978-1-85345-593-3

Acts 13–28 – To the ends of the earth
by Christine Platt

This study guide for the second part of Acts covers Paul's three missionary journeys. See his strategy for urban evangelism and catch his pastoral heart for the fledgling first-century churches. Be challenged by the radical lifestyle of early believers and develop a heart for unreached peoples.
ISBN: 978-1-85345-592-6

The bestselling *Cover to Cover Bible Study* Series

1 Corinthians
Restoring harmony
ISBN: 978-1-85345-374-8

2 Corinthians
Growing a Spirit-filled church
ISBN: 978-1-85345-551-3

1 Timothy
Healthy churches – effective Christians
ISBN: 978-1-85345-291-8

23rd Psalm
The Lord is my shepherd
ISBN: 978-1-85345-449-3

2 Timothy and Titus
Vital Christianity
ISBN: 978-1-85345-338-0

Acts 1–12
Church on the move
ISBN: 978-1-85345-574-2

Acts 13–28
To the ends of the earth
ISBN: 978-1-85345-592-6

Ecclesiastes
Hard questions and spiritual answers
ISBN: 978-1-85345-371-7

Elijah
A man and his God
ISBN: 978-1-85345-575-9

Ephesians
Claiming your inheritance
ISBN: 978-1-85345-229-1

Esther
For such a time as this
ISBN: 978-1-85345-511-7

Fruit of the Spirit
Growing more like Jesus
ISBN: 978-1-85345-375-5

Genesis 1–11
Foundations of reality
ISBN: 978-1-85345-404-2

God's Rescue Plan
Finding God's fingerprints on human history
ISBN: 978-1-85345-294-9

Great Prayers of the Bible
Applying them to our lives today
ISBN: 978-1-85345-253-6

Hebrews
Jesus – simply the best
ISBN: 978-1-85345-337-3

Hosea
The love that never fails
ISBN: 978-1-85345-290-1

Isaiah 1–39
Prophet to the nations
ISBN: 978-1-85345-510-0

Cover to Cover Complete
Read through the Bible chronologically

Take an exciting, year-long journey through the Bible, following events as they happened.

- See God's strategic plan of redemption unfold across the centuries
- Increase your confidence in the Bible as God's inspired message
- Come to know your heavenly Father in a deeper way

The full text of the flowing Holman Christian Standard Bible (HCSB) provides an exhilarating reading experience and is augmented by our beautiful:

- Illustrations
- Maps
- Charts
- Diagrams
- Timeline

And key Scripture verses and devotional thoughts make each day's reading more meaningful.

ISBN: 978-1-85345-433-2

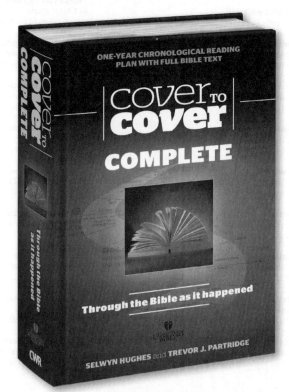